TIGER SHARK

Madeline Nixon

www.av2books.com

Step 1
Go to **www.av2books.com**

Step 2
Enter this unique code
CZPEN8K5O

Step 3
Explore your interactive eBook!

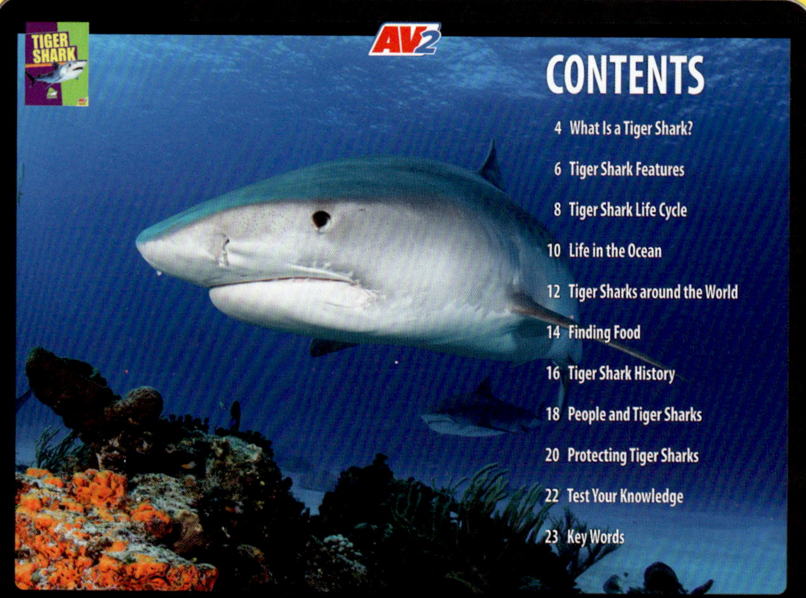

AV2 is optimized for use on any device

Your interactive eBook comes with...

Contents
Browse a live contents page to easily navigate through resources

Audio
Listen to sections of the book read aloud

Videos
Watch informative video clips

Weblinks
Gain additional information for research

Try This!
Complete activities and hands-on experiments

Key Words
Study vocabulary, and complete a matching word activity

Quizzes
Test your knowledge

Slideshows
View images and captions

... and much, much more!

CONTENTS

What Is a Tiger Shark?

Tiger sharks get their name from the dark stripes on their backs. Tiger sharks are not the largest sharks, but they are the second-most dangerous. Tiger sharks, bull sharks, and great white sharks are the three most dangerous sharks. They are called "The Big Three."

“As apex predators, the presence of tiger sharks—and other large sharks—is vital to maintain the proper health and balance of our oceans.”

—Mahmood Shivji, director of the Guy Harvey Research Institute at Nova Southwestern University

Tiger Shark

Scientific Name *Galeocerdo cuvier*

Diet Carnivore

Size 10–16 feet (3–4.9 meters)

Weight 850–1400 pounds (385.6–635 kilograms)

Conservation Status Near Threatened

Population Unknown

Tiger Shark Features

Tiger sharks have several features that help them survive. Some help them hunt. Others help them feed.

Skin

A tiger shark's skin is striped. The stripes fade as the shark grows. They help the shark blend into the ocean floor.

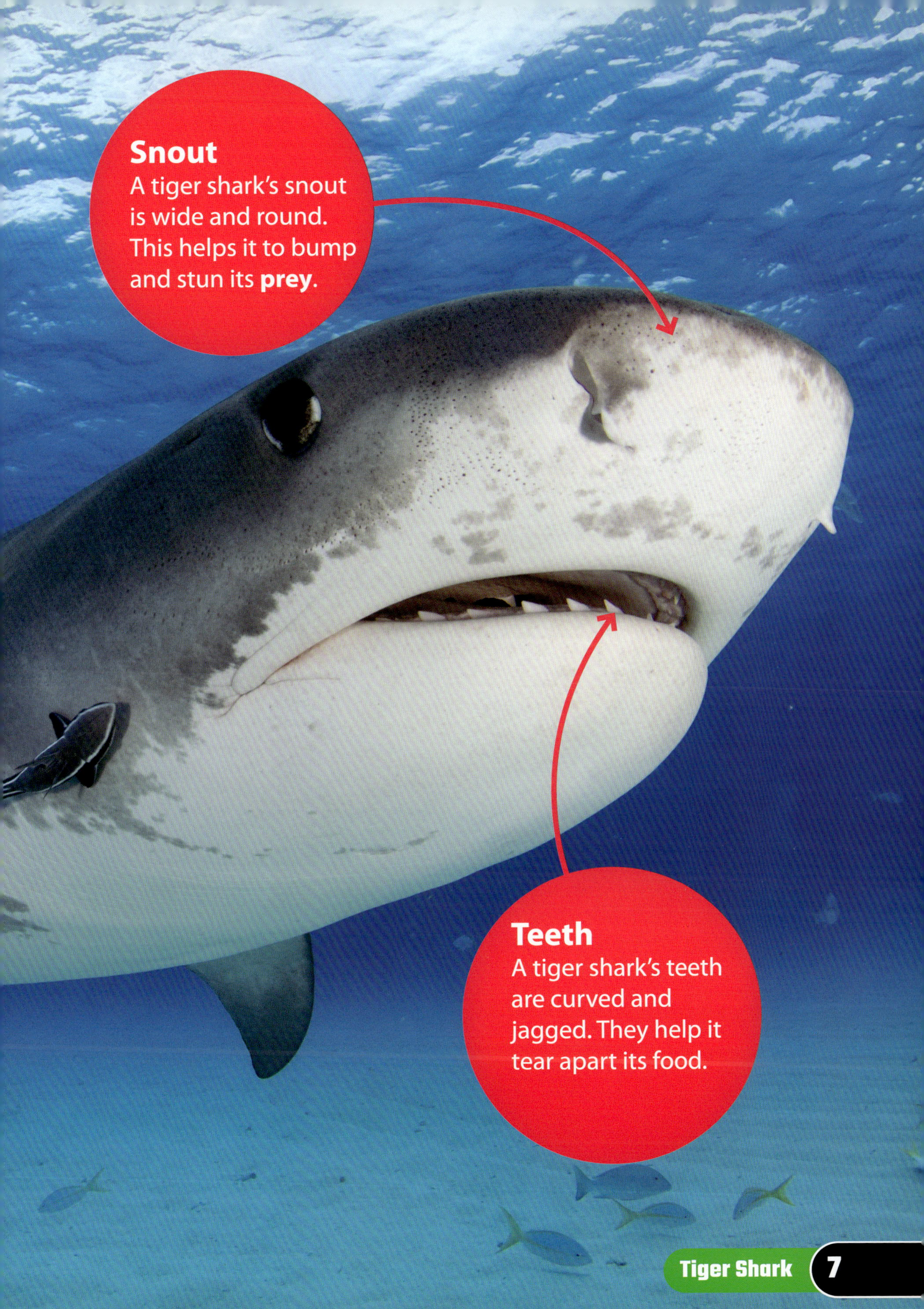
Snout
A tiger shark's snout is wide and round. This helps it to bump and stun its **prey**.
Teeth
A tiger shark's teeth are curved and jagged. They help it tear apart its food.

Tiger Shark Life Cycle

Baby tiger sharks grow in **yolk sacs** inside their mother. They eat the **fluid** inside the sacs. Female tiger sharks give birth to 10 to 82 pups. Tiger sharks are 1.6 to 3.4 feet (50 to 105 centimeters) long when they are born. They live about 27 years.

Tiger sharks grow very slowly. Males are adults once they are 7 to 9 feet (2.1 to 2.7 m) long. Females are adults at 8 to 10 feet (2.4 to 3 m).

How Big Are Sharks?

Human
5.5 feet (1.7 m)

Blacktip Shark
8 feet (2.4 m)

Bull Shark
11.5 feet (3.5 m)

Shortfin Mako Shark
12 feet (3.7 m)

Tiger Shark
16 feet (4.9 m)

Great Hammerhead Shark
20 feet (6.1 m)

Great White Shark
20 feet (6.1 m)

Whale Shark
32 feet (9.8 m)

Life in the Ocean

Tiger sharks like warm water. They usually live near coastlines and other shallow waters. The deepest they will go is about 1,150 feet (350 m). Tiger sharks live in **tropical** waters during winter months. In the summer, they **migrate** north.

Tiger sharks are **nocturnal**. This means they hunt at night. They spend most of the day in deeper waters. At night, they hunt for food near the shore.

SHARK BITES

Tiger sharks **move** around a lot. Some will **travel** up to **9.9 miles (16 kilometers)** in a **single day**.

Tiger Sharks around the World

Tiger sharks live off the coasts of most continents and islands. They are not usually found in the open ocean. During colder months, tiger sharks stay close to the **equator**.

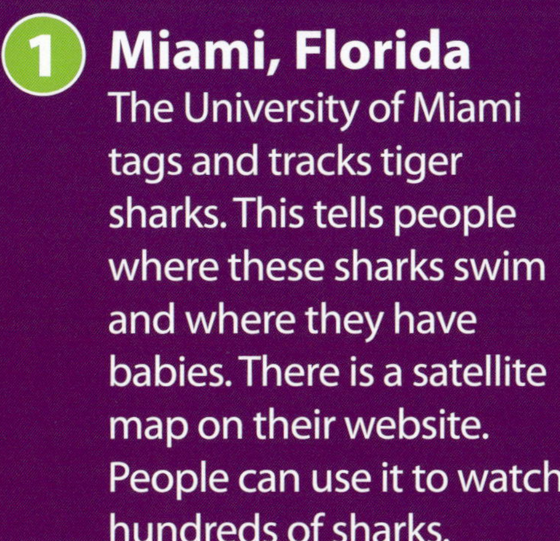

1 Miami, Florida

The University of Miami tags and tracks tiger sharks. This tells people where these sharks swim and where they have babies. There is a satellite map on their website. People can use it to watch hundreds of sharks.

2 Iceland

Tiger sharks follow warm **gulf streams**. Sometimes, they swim as far north as Iceland.

3 Tubbataha Reefs Natural Park, Philippines

Many tiger sharks live at the Tubbataha Reefs Natural Park. It is a **UNESCO World Heritage Site**. All wildlife is protected there.

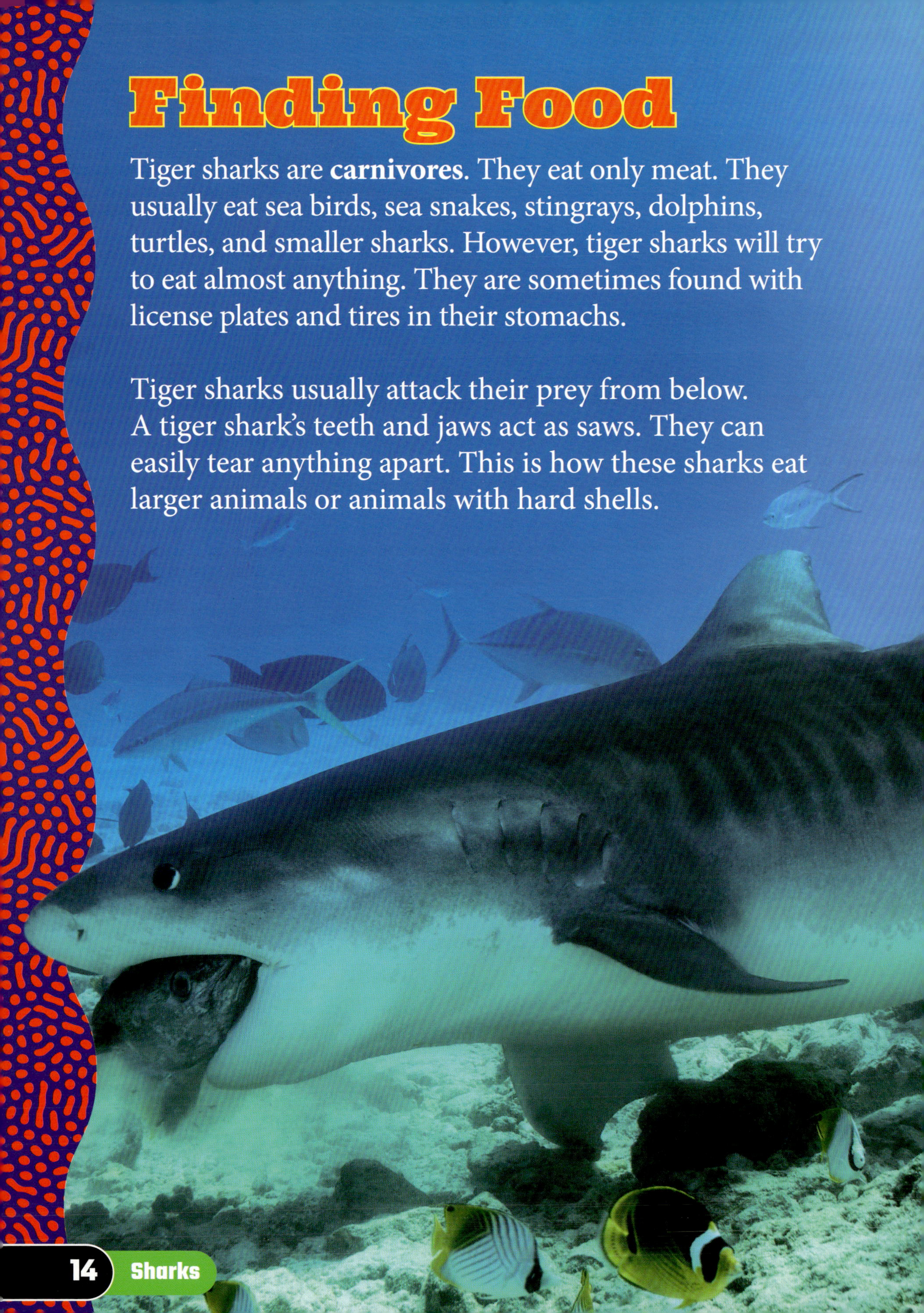

Finding Food

Tiger sharks are **carnivores**. They eat only meat. They usually eat sea birds, sea snakes, stingrays, dolphins, turtles, and smaller sharks. However, tiger sharks will try to eat almost anything. They are sometimes found with license plates and tires in their stomachs.

Tiger sharks usually attack their prey from below. A tiger shark's teeth and jaws act as saws. They can easily tear anything apart. This is how these sharks eat larger animals or animals with hard shells.

SHARK BITES

One tiger shark was found with **two cans**, **two burlap sacks**, and a **bottle** in its stomach.

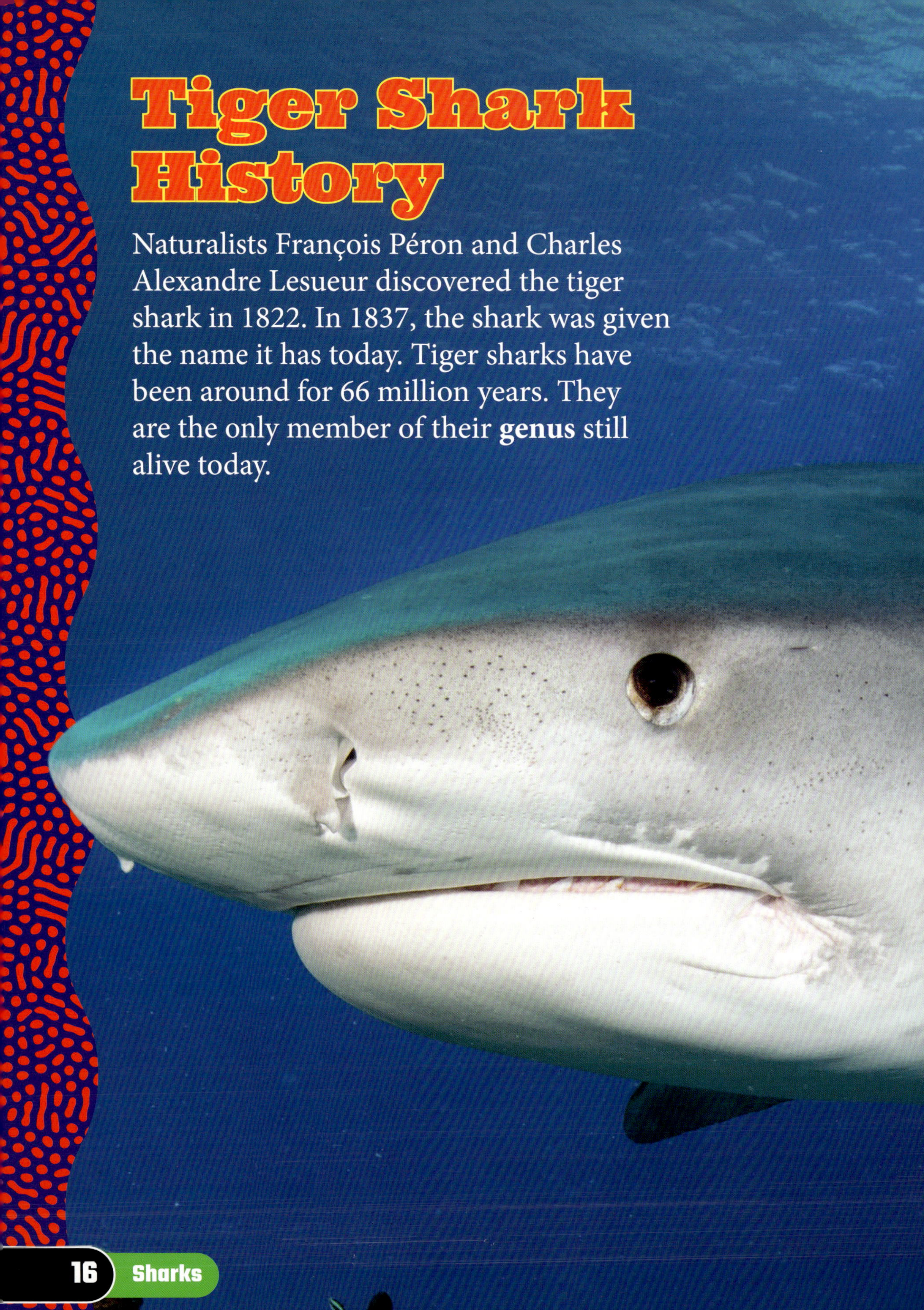

Tiger Shark History

Naturalists François Péron and Charles Alexandre Lesueur discovered the tiger shark in 1822. In 1837, the shark was given the name it has today. Tiger sharks have been around for 66 million years. They are the only member of their **genus** still alive today.

There used to be 11 sharks in the same genus as tiger sharks.

People and Tiger Sharks

Tiger sharks can be dangerous to humans. Their teeth and jaws are powerful. One bite can lead to death. Unlike great white sharks, they do not swim away after biting. However, there are fewer tiger shark attacks than great white shark attacks. Many people like to swim with tiger sharks. Tiger Beach in the Bahamas is one of the best places to do this.

Tiger sharks have only one predator in the ocean. Groups of orcas hunt them. Tiger sharks are also fished around the world. People catch them for their fins, skin, and livers. Hawai'ians use the skin for drums.

SHARK BITES
Tiger sharks are the **third most commonly caught** shark.

Protecting Tiger Sharks

Tiger sharks are being overfished. They are not **extinct** yet. However, scientists think their numbers are going down. Soon, they may become endangered.

Several places protect the tiger shark. It is **illegal** to fish and sell tiger sharks in Florida. Tiger sharks are also protected in Australia. Scientists tag tiger sharks so they can study them. By learning more about these fish, they can help protect them.

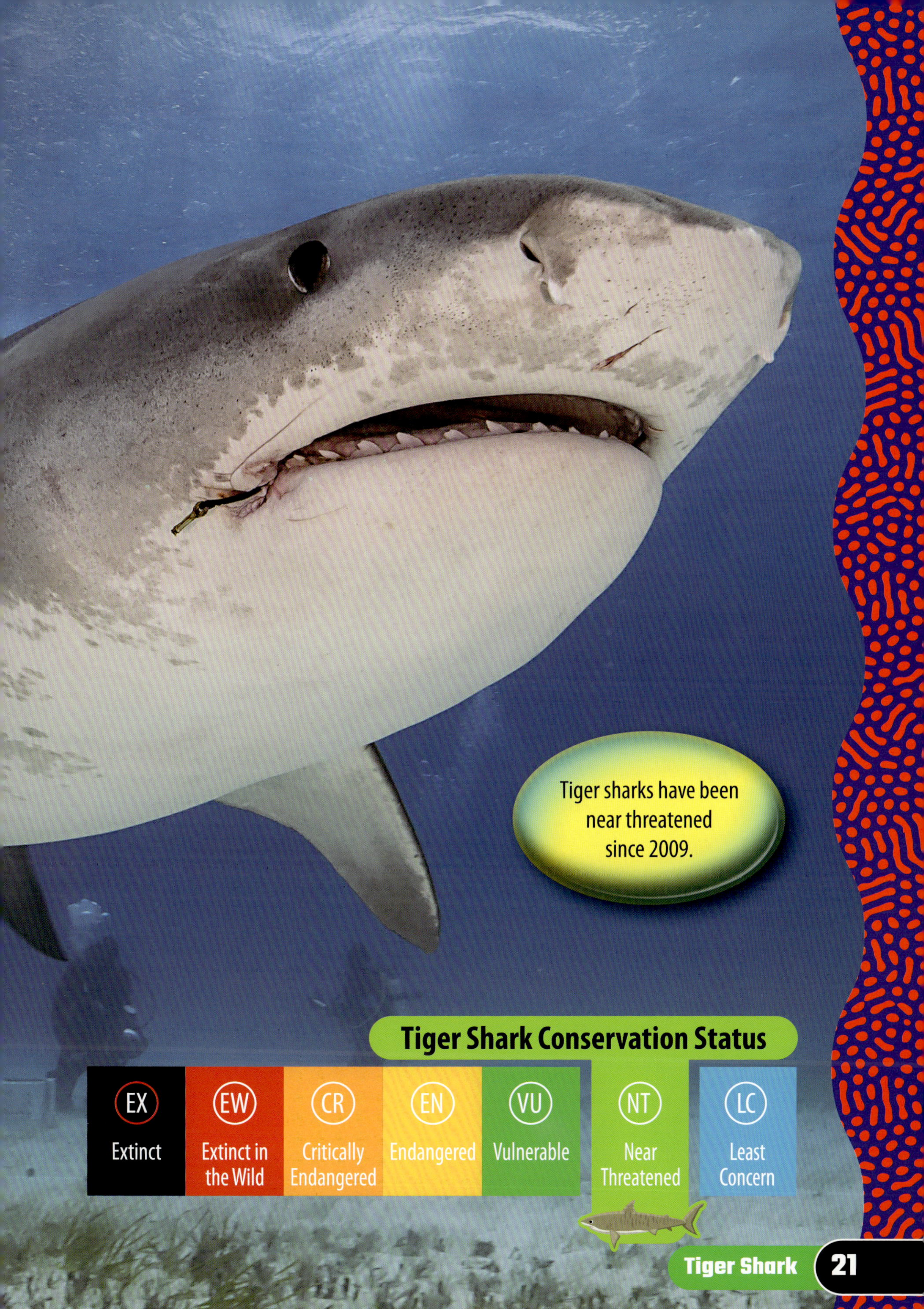
Tiger sharks have been near threatened since 2009.
Tiger Shark Conservation Status
EX Extinct
EW Extinct in the Wild
CR Critically Endangered
EN Endangered
VU Vulnerable
NT Near Threatened
LC Least Concern

Test Your Knowledge

1
Where do tiger sharks sometimes travel when following gulf streams?

Iceland

2
Which state has made it illegal to hunt and sell tiger sharks?

Florida

3
How long have tiger sharks existed?

66 million years

4
What non-food items are sometimes found in tiger shark stomachs?

Bottles, burlap sacks, cans, license plates, and tires

5
Where do tiger sharks get their name from?

The dark stripes on their back

6
How many pups can a female tiger shark give birth to?

10 to 82

7
Which park in the Philippines is a UNESCO World Heritage Site?

Tubbataha Reefs Natural Park

8
How long do tiger sharks live?

About 27 years

Key Words

carnivores: animals that eat only meat

equator: a line dividing Earth into northern and southern halves

extinct: no longer living on Earth

fluid: any liquid, such as water

genus: a group of animals that are closely related to each other

gulf streams: warm ocean currents that flow north from Mexico

illegal: against the law

migrate: to move from one place to another

nocturnal: awake at night

prey: an animal that is hunted by another animal

tropical: places near the equator

UNESCO World Heritage Site: a landmark or protected zone that cannot be touched or destroyed

yolk sacs: gooey liquid surrounding babies inside their mothers

Index

Get the best of both worlds.

AV2 bridges the gap between print and digital.

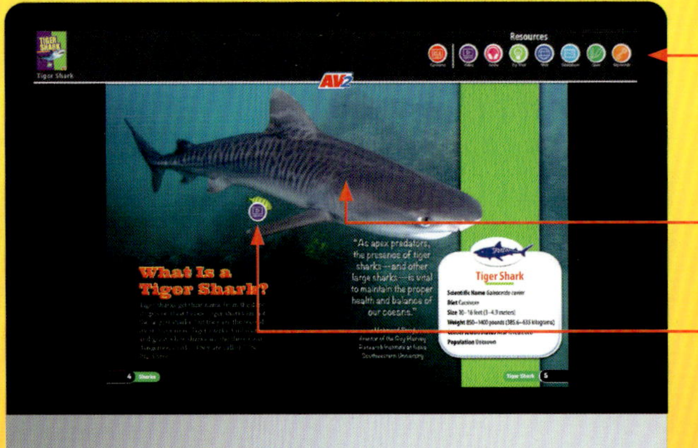

The expandable resources toolbar enables quick access to content including **videos**, **audio**, **activities**, **weblinks**, **slideshows**, **quizzes**, and **key words**.

Animated videos make static images come alive.

Resource icons on each page help readers to further **explore key concepts**.

Published by AV2
350 5th Avenue, 59th Floor
New York, NY 10118
Website: www.av2books.com

Library of Congress Control Number: 2019955084

ISBN 978-1-7911-2119-8 (hardcover)
ISBN 978-1-7911-2120-4 (softcover)
ISBN 978-1-7911-2121-1 (multi-user eBook)
ISBN 978-1-7911-2122-8 (single-user eBook)

Printed in Guangzhou, China
1 2 3 4 5 6 7 8 9 0 24 23 22 21 20

022020
101119

Project Coordinator: John Willis
Designer: Terry Paulhus

AV2 acknowledges Alamy, Minden Pictures, and Shutterstock as its primary image suppliers for this title.